Our Changing World

Program Authors

Connie Juel, Ph.D.

Jeanne R. Paratore, Ed.D.

Deborah Simmons, Ph.D.

Sharon Vaughn, Ph.D.

ISBN 0-328-21459-0

PEARSON
Scott Foresman

2 3 4 5 6 7 8 9 10 V011 12 11 10 09 08 07 06

Editorial Offices: Glenview, Illinois • Parsippany, New Jersey • New York, New York
Sales Offices: Boston, Massachusetts • Duluth, Georgia • Glenview, Illinois
Coppell, Texas • Sacramento, California • Mesa, Arizona

Our Changing World

Contents

When Things Change

See page 35 for My New Words!

When Things Change

If families must move to a new home, kids can get sad. They will miss all their pals and neighbors. What can make them happy?

This kid hugs his dog and talks to it. That makes him smile.

This girl gets her ball and bat and plans fun games with new pals. That makes her happy!

This family cuts small parts off Mom's old dress, Dad's torn vest, and Jeff's worn scarf. They use these cloth patches and more to make a quilt.

Families can hang quilts on walls in their new homes. These quilts help them think of fun times they had.

This small, shiny thing can help kids who
move think of pals. Kids can get this at the mall.
They can paste a pal's photo in it.

When kids miss pals, they can look at pals'
happy faces. This will make them smile and think
of fun times when they are gone.

Kids can save photos in albums.

Kids can snap photos of parks where they had fun ball games with groups of buddies. They can snap their school too.

Kids can even snap the corner store where they promise Mom and Dad that they will get just one yummy snack!

Taking Pictures

by Lakshmi Patel

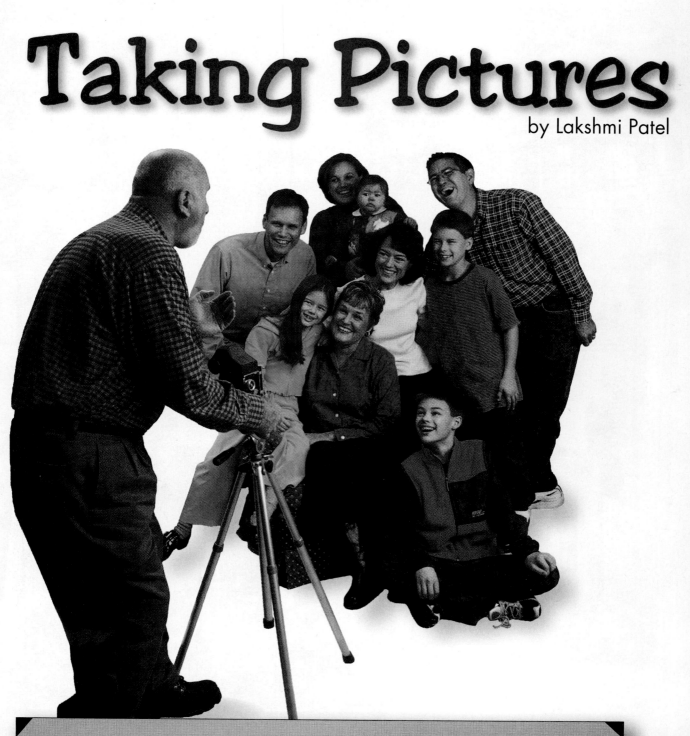

Did you ever take pictures with a camera? Did you pose for pictures with Mom and Dad or with your best pals?

Did you know that in past times people did not take pictures?

Before cameras were invented, artists made pictures. Dads, moms, and kids sat in groups while artists worked. Granddads and grandmoms posed as well.

Artists did a nice job. In their art, kids had fun with games, blocks, or balls.

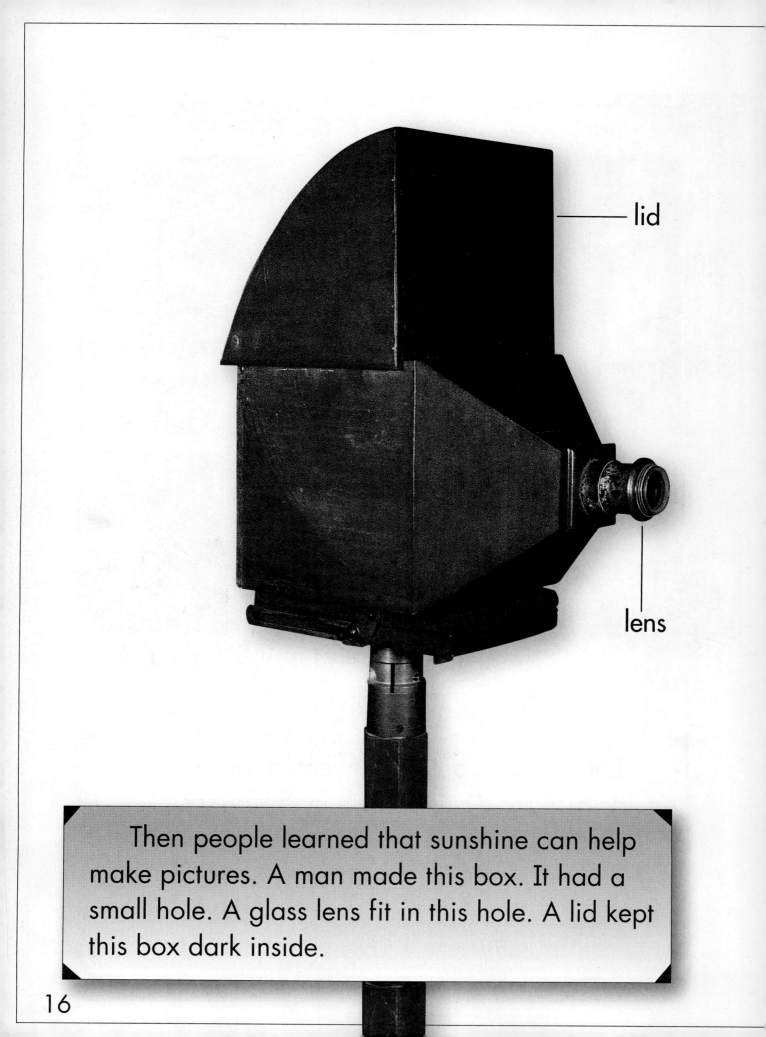

lid

lens

Then people learned that sunshine can help make pictures. A man made this box. It had a small hole. A glass lens fit in this hole. A lid kept this box dark inside.

When sunshine came in the small hole, it made a picture on the back wall. But this picture did not last long. It was gone at sunset.

copper plate
fits here

copper plate

lens

First photos were made on thin copper plates with silver on them. A small copper plate fit inside a box. This made a camera.

This man set up his camera by this girl. She sat still as he let sunshine in the box. This made a picture on the thin copper plate inside. The man took the copper plate out.

Then the girl placed this small photo in glass, framed it, and hung it on the wall.

35mm camera

camera phone

digital camera

35mm SLR camera

disposable camera

Now cameras are quite small, and pictures are made into prints. They are fun to save and look at in albums or on computers.

Kids can take pictures to remember fun times. Kids can snap pals at baseball games, campfires, and parties. Kids can snap neighbors smiling and waving.

And if pals move, kids can promise to take and send pictures.

21

A New Tune for TIM

by Mara Lewis   illustrated by David Opie

Mom, Dad, and Tim talk at supper. The family must move soon. Dad got a job in New York. Mom tells Tim that life in New York is fun.

"Can I take my trumpet to New York?" asks Tim. "I promise that you can take it with you," Mom tells him. But Tim is sad. He will miss making songs with his pals in band class.

Tim tells his pals he must move. All his buddies tell Tim they will miss him when he is gone.

Then Tim's pals, Lin and Ricky, think of a way to surprise him. They tell this idea to Miss Hall. She thinks it is a good plan.

Miss Hall tells the plan to the rest of the class. All the kids grin. Tim will like this plan! What do you think it is?

When Tim gets to band class, all his pals smile at him.

Miss Hall grins, "It's time for our new song. It's called 'A Tune for Tim.'"

Lin bangs on her drums and Ricky sings. Kids clap and snap.

Tim picks up his trumpet and starts to jam. He is happy that his pals made a song just for him.

Soon it is time for Mom, Dad, and Tim to move. Tim is sad, but he hums the tune his pals made for him. It makes him less sad.

Tim helps Mom and Dad pack up rugs, dishpans, and big pots.

Then a big van drives up. It parks on the drive by the backyard. Strong men fill the van with boxes.

"Let's go," Dad tells Tim. "It's time!"

Tim walks to the car and gets inside. He hugs his trumpet.

Tim thinks New York is nice, but he misses his old home and his classmates.

Mom smiles, "Look, Tim."

Tim looks.

Neighbor kids are making songs on the sidewalk! One kid has a flute. One has a drum. Tim rushes over. He makes tunes on his trumpet. The kids all grin.

"My name is Roxy," smiles the girl
with the flute. "You are a trumpet champ!"
Tim grins. "Can I make songs with
this group?"

Roxy nods. Then she asks, "What is the name of your song?"

Tim hugs his trumpet and smiles, "'A Tune for Tim and His New York Pals!'"

My Favorite Things

Raindrops on roses and whiskers on kittens,
Bright copper kettles and warm woolen mittens,
Brown paper packages tied up with strings,
These are a few of my favorite things.
When the dog bites, when the bee stings,
When I'm feeling sad,
I simply remember my favorite things,
And then I don't feel so bad.

My New Words

album
An **album** is a book for photos.

gone
He has **gone** to a movie.

group
A **group** is a number of people or things together.

move
When you **move**, you go from one place to another.

neighbor
A **neighbor** is someone who lives near you.

photo
A **photo** is a picture you make with a camera. It is a shorter word for *photograph*.

promise
To **promise** is to say that you will or will not do something.

Contents

From Seed to Plant

See page 63 for My New Words!

From Seed to Plant

Can you plant pansies? Yes! Here's how. Get a clay pot and fill it with dirt. Get a bunch of pansy seeds. Plant the pansy seeds in the dirt. Place the pot in a sunny place.

Water the dirt often. Let water drain from the pot. Green stems will spring up.

Soon buds will form on the stems. In time, these buds will change into pansies.

Farmers on the plains plant corn. They place seeds, called kernels, in dirt. Sun shines. Rain falls. In about five days, frail stems pop up. Stems turn into small cornstalks. Cornstalks get tall, up to a farmer's waist.

Tassels form on top. Cobs of corn, hidden inside husks, pop out.

Now the stalks are so tall that they are almost above this farmer. This farmer picks corn when it is ripe.

Did you know that some grapes have seeds inside? Farmers plant these seeds and wait for them to become vines. Farmers plant vines in straight lines on hills. These vines twist around wire railings.

Days and days pass. Bunches of grapes hang on trailing vines. These small, hard grapes get big and ripe. Farmers snip off bunches and fill pails with grapes. Then we can eat them!

WHAT PLANT WILL THIS BE?

by Gilbert Foreman

These seeds are flat and white. Dig holes and plant these seeds in a sunny spot. These seeds like lots and lots of sun! They need rain often too. What will we get?

seed

pumpkin

All these came from those flat, white seeds.
Each has seeds inside and a short, fat stem.
Deep lines run up and down their hard shells.
Did you ever eat treats made with these?

These seeds may seem big. They are called pits or stones. They have small holes and a red tint. Plant them in straight lines. What will these seeds become?

peach

seed

See this peach tree? It came from those seeds.
It is not a very big tree. It has fuzzy peaches on
its branches. The peaches are almost ripe.

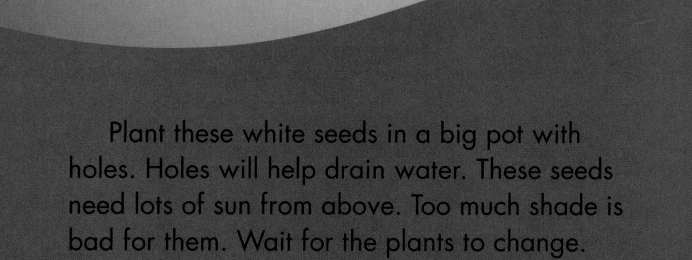

Plant these white seeds in a big pot with holes. Holes will help drain water. These seeds need lots of sun from above. Too much shade is bad for them. Wait for the plants to change.

lemon

seed

This came from those white seeds. It has green leaves. Yellow is peeking out from the leaves! Cut a few of these and squeeze them. Add water. Make a nice drink for a hot day.

Plant these small, black seeds in wet dirt
with lots of sun. Keep weeds away. In about six
days green leaves will pop up. Soon leaves will
be vines.

watermelon

seed

See how this seed has changed! This has a hard green shell. Cut a slice of this and eat it. The soft red part is sweet! Cut slices for your pals. Yum! Yum! Yum!

Garden Art

by Kim Mather
illustrated by Adam Gustavson

"I like walking outside in spring, Granddad," said Ken. "The sun shines from above. Trees turn green, and leaves pop out on branches."

"Yes, spring is a time of change," Granddad said. "Birds sing in trees, and streams fill with rainwater. Days get long. In spring, I get green plants for my garden."

"Granddad, your garden is different from other gardens. Why is it like this?" asked Ken. Granddad's garden had rocks and hills. Small fish played in its streams. Thin reeds swayed in soft breezes.

"You will often see gardens like this in my homeland across the seas," said Granddad.

Granddad turned to Ken. "Do you see this little tree, Ken? It is in the best spot in the garden."

"What is it?" asked Ken.

"It's a tree that stays small," said Granddad.

"It is not tall like that pine tree."

"Why does it stay small?" asked Ken.

"I trim the main stem and cut stray leaves," said Granddad. "I wait for it to reach straight up, almost to my waist. Then I cut off its top. Days and weeks pass. Green branches pop out. I pick five to save and cut the rest."

"See how those five branches fan out from
the tree?" Granddad said.

"How did you get them to bend that way?"
Ken asked.

"I trained each branch," smiled Granddad.
"I used twine and wire to make them stay. I let
small leaves pop up and cut off the rest."

"Are you an artist, Granddad?" asked Ken.
Granddad smiled, "It takes an artist to make a
little tree like this. It is for all to enjoy. It is art for
a garden."

"This tree makes me feel happy," grinned
Ken. "I like garden art."

Riddle Time

1. What does a baby ear of corn call its father?

2. How do you fix a broken tomato?

3. Why did the farmer plant seeds in a pond?

4. What kind of beans never grow in a garden?

1. Popcorn 2. with tomato paste 3. He wanted to grow watermelons. 4. jellybeans

My New Words

above   The sun is **above** the trees.

almost   I **almost** missed the bus.

change   To **change** means to make or become different.

frail   If something is **frail**, it is thin and not very strong.

husk   The **husk** is the outside leaves covering an ear of corn.

often   It snows **often** in January.

reed   A **reed** is a kind of tall grass that grows in wet places.

straight If something is **straight**, it does not bend, turn, or curve.

tassel   A **tassel** is a hanging bunch of threads. Each ear of corn has a **tassel**.

Contents

Animals

See page 95 for My New Words!

Animals

When this cat was born, he looked like his mom, only smaller. His eyes stayed closed. All he did was eat and sleep and cry. As a small kitten, he ran and played in a field.

He was happiest when he chased mice. Now he is a big cat, covered with lots of soft fur. He spends each day sleeping in the warm sun. He is the sleepiest cat.

This chick started life inside an egg. Her mom sat on it and kept it warm. The chick cracked the eggshell with her beak. A wet ball popped out. She did not look like her mom at all. This chick looked messier than a wet mop!

When this chick was drier, she seemed like a fluffy ball. She chirped and scratched for grain. Peep, peep! This chick got much bigger. She is a hen like her mom now.

At birth, this panda was small and pink. Time passed, and this little panda changed. He turned into a frisky cub with black and white fur. This cub ate green stalks, just like his mom.

This cub got bigger and friskier. Now he is a huge panda. He looks like his mom. This big panda will leave his mom's den. He will live in a den by himself and find stalks and stems to eat. Now he is bigger than his mom!

This animal was born small and had pink skin. She stayed safe and warm in her mom's pocket. Isn't that the funniest way to be carried?

In time, this tot jumped from the pocket and hopped next to her mom. She ate grass and drank from streams. Now she is six feet tall! She lives in a country far from us. What is this animal's name?

A Safe Place for Animals

by Monica Carr

This huge park is in the country. It is far from places where most people live. Its big hills have the snowiest tops around. Tall trees grow up the hillsides.

Many animals roam in this park. Big birds fly above green fields. Fish swim in flowing streams. Animals drink fresh water from these streams.

Each day park vets drive on the park's dirt roads. They check paths for lost or hurt animals. Vets care for these animals. Vets keep them safe from harm and treat them if they are sick.

Vets see a cub by the road. He is moaning in pain and may be lost. If his mom is not close by, vets will load this cub into a van. They will get this cub the help he needs.

Vets will feed this cub warm milk. Vets will check for cuts or crushed bones. Vets will clean him with soap and water. Vets will place soft blankets in his bed and cover him. Each day this cub will get better.

When this cub is stronger, vets will drive him to a safer place in the park. This place has trees and streams where he can swim and fish. It has a wall around it that will help keep him safe. This cub will stay until he is all better.

Vets will keep checking on this cub. He will get bigger and faster. He will grow into a huge animal. Vets will make sure that he can live on his own and take care of himself.

In time, this grown cub will not need the wall. He will be free to roam in the park. He will be safer and happier than ever. The vets will be glad that they helped.

A TADPOLE'S TALE

by Sheri Slevin
illustrated by Kevin Rechin

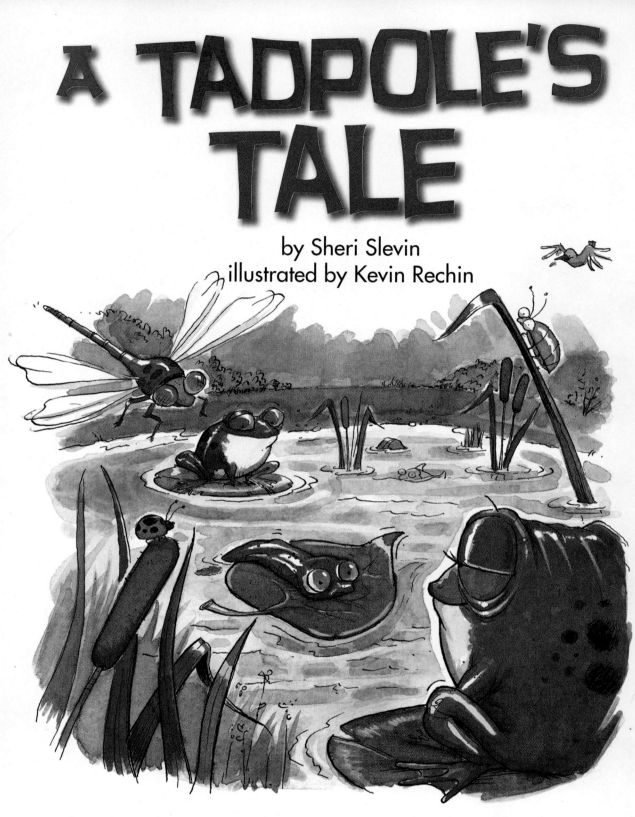

Tad hatched from an egg. He is only two days old. He sticks on weeds and grasses that help him float on this pond. His tail will grow. Soon he will use his long tail to swim.

Tad is sad. He does not look like Mom
and Dad. Tad is missing those arms that let Mom
pick him up for big hugs. Tad is missing those
strong legs that help Dad hop faster across fields.

"I cannot be the strongest and fastest frog in the country with no arms or legs!" Tad moans to Dad.

Dad just smiles. He jumps from leaf to leaf in the warm sun. "Do not worry," he tells Tad. But Tad is still sad.

Two weeks pass and Tad grows. He can swim faster than his pals. Still, Tad has only a tail.

Tad's pals ask, "When will you grow arms and legs so you can jump like your mom and dad?"

"I don't know," Tad tells them. "But I do have teeth now. And I eat bigger plants." But Tad does not feel better. With no arms or legs, he is just getting sadder.

Weeks pass. Tad's legs are growing, but they are short and weak. "Dad, I have got the funniest legs and still no arms," Tad groans.
Dad just smiles. "Do not worry, Tad."

More weeks pass. Now Tad has arms too. Will Tad be like Dad? Dad can swim in water and hop on land. He can run for cover from snakes and big fish. All the small animals know Dad is the fastest frog.

Tad is now 12 weeks old. Dad thinks that
Tad has grown enough. "Leap on this floating
leaf," Dad tells Tad. Tad leaps. Tad makes it!

Tad is happy! Tad sits by Dad on the leaf. Tad looks at himself in the water. He can see two frogs side by side. Both have long arms and legs.

"I am happier than ever," Tad grins at Dad.
"I look just like my mom and dad. And I got
arms and legs just in time for that Jumping Show
today. I will jump my best and fastest."

Leap! Leap! Leap! Tad did it! Tad jumped better and faster than the others. He is the winner of the Jumping Show. Tad is the happiest frog in the pond. He can jump like Dad and hug Mom back.

Animal Family Names

Bear
FATHER | boar
MOTHER | sow
BABY | cub

Deer
FATHER | buck
MOTHER | doe
BABY | fawn

Horse
FATHER | stallion
MOTHER | mare
BABY | foal, colt, or filly

Sheep
FATHER | ram
MOTHER | ewe
BABY | lamb

What other animal family names do you know?

94

My New Words

animal
Any living thing that can move about is an **animal**.

country
The **country** is the land outside the city. A **country** is also the land and a group of people with the same leader.

cover
When you **cover** something, you put something else over it. A **cover** is anything that protects or hides.

field
A **field** is a piece of land without trees.

frisky
If something is **frisky**, it is playful.

panda
A **panda** is a large black and white animal that looks like a bear.

pocket
You can put things in a **pocket**.

warm
If something is **warm**, it is more hot than cold.

Contents

What Changes Are Hard?

See page 125 for My New Words!

What Changes Are Hard?

by Anton Hill

Daisy is not happy. She has to start classes at a new school.

"No one will like me!" Daisy moaned. "What if kids make fun of me? What if kids won't talk to me?"

Mom sighed. "Daisy, you are fun and nice. It will be all right. The children will like you." Mom helped Daisy tie her laces. "It is time to go."

Daisy tugged on her backpack. She kicked the sidewalk below her feet as she walked. She felt like she might cry. When the school was in sight, she slowed down.

Daisy looked up high at the school. She held on tight to her backpack. Daisy thought, "This is an important day. I will smile and be nice. I will make friends."

Daisy stepped into the bright hallway. It was full of kids. One child greeted Daisy.

"You must be new," she said. "My name is Grace. Can I help you?"

Daisy smiled her shy smile. "Thanks," she said. "I will be in Miss Roan's class."

"I am in Miss Roan's class!" cried Grace. "We are in the same class. I will take you to meet her."

Grace led Daisy to her class. Grace said,
"Miss Roan, this is Daisy. She will be in this
class. Isn't that lucky?"

Miss Roan smiled. "We feel happy that you'll
be in this class, Daisy."

That night, Daisy felt happier. She told her mom, "It was hard going to a new school. But you were right. It was fine. I met Grace. I think I might like it."

The Great Chicago Fire!

by Alex Jordan

On a fall day in 1871, Chicago's night sky
turned bright red.
"FIRE!" a man yelled.
In a flash, flames leaped high in the sky.

High winds made fire race through miles and miles of streets. Flames burned homes and stores. Churches and banks burned. Walls fell. Land quaked below people's feet. People ran from this raging fire.

Moms, dads, and children jammed the streets. Men used ropes and dragged trunks full of things they had saved. Kids grabbed things that might help them feel less sad. One smart child dressed in her dresses, pants, and shirts all at the same time.

Fires burned for days. Smoke turned the sky gray and dirty. When the last fires died, lots of things would not be the same.

Many families lost homes. People from other places sent coats, and things to eat and drink. Important places, such as schools, had turned to dust and ashes. Kids had no way to learn. People sent things that kids needed. That helped.

1890

Today

This fire had burned lots and lots of homes and stores. But the people of Chicago did not give up. In days, they started to build homes and stores again. They made Chicago a bigger, safer, and better place.

Coal's New Home

by Bridget Brighton
illustrated by Mary Roja

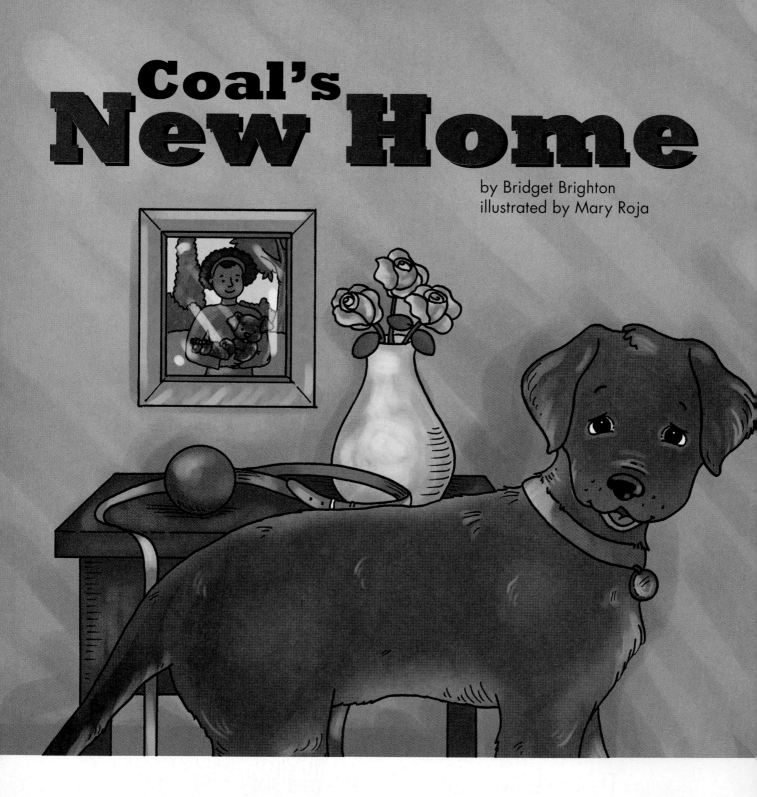

I am Coal. Joan and I live in this tall building on High Street. I play with my bright red ball and my rubber bone all day. At night, Joan walks me in the park below.

Slam! Click! Click! Joan's high heels click on the tile. She's home! I wag my tail. I am happy that Joan is home.

But Joan seems sad. She hugs me tight and cries, "Coal, I got a new job and must move to a new home. I can't keep pets in my new home, so I can't take you with me."

"You will have a new home, Coal. You will like it. You will run and play. I will miss you," Joan sighed.

It is important that I show Joan that I will miss her too. I lick her cheek.

Joan pets me and takes me outside. A man
with a van smiles at us and takes my leash. Joan
hugs me tight. She tells me I will be fine.

I get in this van with the man and lie still. He drives away. Where will we go? Will my new home be nice? The man reaches back and pats me. He whispers, "My kids will like you, Coal!" Kids? My new home might be fun!

After a long drive, the van stops. It is time to meet my family. Three children peek in the van and smile at me.

"How was your trip, Coal?" a child asks.
"I'm Jay. This is Neal, and this is Gail. We feel
so happy to meet you, Coal."

I get out of the van. The sun is bright.

"Look, Coal," Jay cries.

What a sight! I see a big lake and a red barn
full of hay. All around I see green hills.

"Run, run!" these kids yell and grin.

I race up high hills. I pass hens fighting for grains of corn. I race back to the kids. They clap. Jay beams. "Coal, you run fast! You can run faster than we can."

On a bright day these kids take me to the lake.
"Try swimming, Coal!" Gail begs.

I had not swum before, so I am filled with
fright. But when Jay throws a big stick far into the
lake, I dive in! Swimming is fun!

My life has changed! I race each morning and each night. I chase hens and play with kids. And I swim in a big lake under sunny skies. Joan was right. I DO like my new home!

I Miss My Old Friends

My New Words

beam When you **beam**, you smile brightly.

below His room is **below** mine.

Chicago **Chicago** is a big city in Illinois.

child A **child** is a young boy or girl.

children **Children** are young boys and girls.

full If something is **full**, it cannot hold any more.

important Something that is **important** has a lot of meaning or worth.

quake If you feel something **quake**, you feel it shake.

Contents

Weather Changes

Weather

It's a sunny day at the beach. But in a moment it gets dark, and it's not even late in the day. What does it mean? See up in the sky?

Changes

Large gray clouds grow bigger. Paper blows by. Can you hear thunder? Even though it would be fun to stay, it is time to go. Rain begins to splash. Cover your poor head and run inside!

This is a big storm. Black clouds speed across the wide sky. Winds race. Crash! Trees fall. Rain splatters. Water in the river rises. It may wash over its bank. See that funnel cloud? Sirens wail to tell us to get to a safe place.

Open this up. Run down these steps. It is safe and cozy in here. Wait until the storm passes. It spins by fast.

Hush! Is the storm over? We are safe. Let's go back up to the top.

It is chilly. Clouds hang low. Snowflakes flutter. Then they fall faster and faster. Wind blows and spins white snow into high drifts. It is hard to see far. This is a big snowstorm.

Snow piles high against houses and windows. Cars slide on ice. It is not safe to drive. The river freezes. Ice hangs from tree branches. Ice and snow are all around!

Neighbors can help clean up snow. Cars start
up. It is safe to drive again. Kids make snowmen,
skate on frozen lakes, or sled down hills.

Storms can change what is around us. It is important that we stay safe. But when the storm ends, we can clean up, and we can have fun.

What Will

by Kathy Domke • illustrated by Peggy Mozley

Look out these windows. Is it raining? Is it sunny? Is it snowing? If you play outside in the rain, sun, or snow, what will you need?

You Need?

What will keep us dry when it is raining?
What will protect us in the hot, hot sun? What
will keep us toasty and dry when it is snowing?

Raindrops start to fall. Katy will play outside with Alan. What will she need?

This large umbrella will keep Katy dry. It will protect her head from falling rain.

Poor Alan is walking in rain. Where is his umbrella?

Look at Alan's glasses. Have you ever seen glasses like these before? These can wipe and wash off his glasses. They can help him see.

The sun is shining bright and hot. Katy will play outside with Alan. What will she need? This sunscreen will protect Katy's skin in the hot, hot sun. Even though she will be in shade at times, she puts on sunscreen.

Alan is in the hot sun. What will he need?
Look at Alan's backpack. Have you ever
seen a backpack like this before? This clever
backpack helps keep water close by. Water
helps Alan in the hot sun.

Snow has fallen all day long. Brrr! Katy will play outside. What will she need?

This cozy coat, thick scarf, and a pair of fuzzy mittens will keep Katy toasty and dry. A fuzzy hat protects her head.

Alan is walking in the snow. Why doesn't he shiver? Where is his face?

Look at Alan's hat. Have you ever seen a hat like his before? This hat covers all of Alan's head and much of his face. This hat will protect Alan.

Katy and Alan play outside in rain, sun, and snow. No matter what it is like outside, they know what they will need.

Do you? What if you play outside in rain, sun, or snow? What will you need?

NORTH WIND AND SUN

by Justin Mason
illustrated by Stephen Alcorn

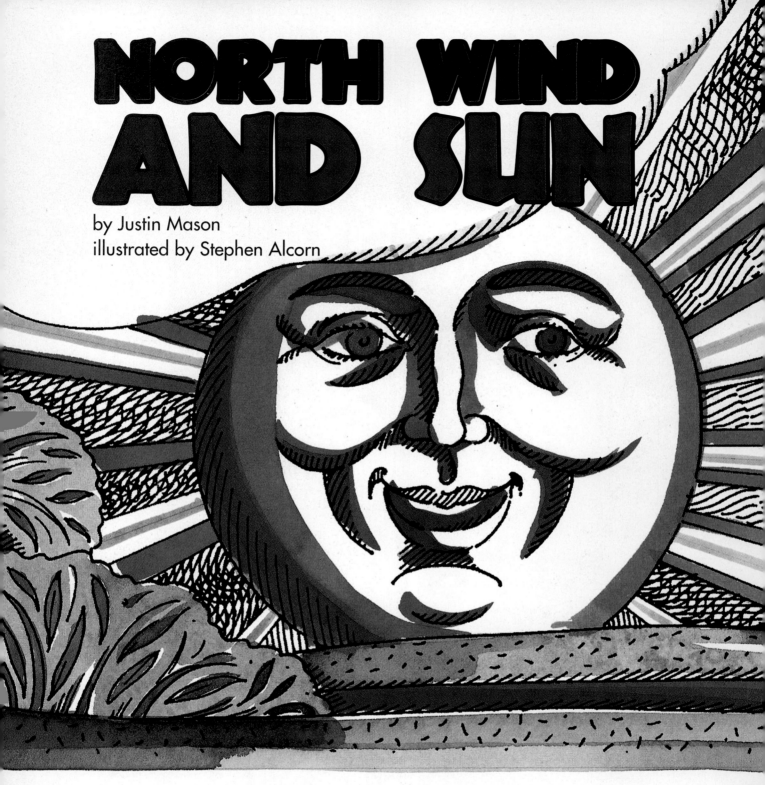

"I am strong," bragged North Wind. "I am even stronger than Sun!"

"No, I am stronger," bragged Sun.

So North Wind and Sun had a contest to see who is stronger.

North Wind and Sun waited until a lady walked by. She had on a coat. A large pink hat sat on her head.

"See that lady?" asked Sun. "I bet I can make her take her hat off."

"I am clever," bragged North Wind. "I will win this contest in just one moment. I will blow her hat off!"

North Wind huffed and puffed.

Lemons dropped off trees! Robins clung to branches! Spiders grabbed their webs! Could North Wind even make the river wash away?

The lady shivered in the chill. She clutched her coat and tugged her hat on tight. She had never felt such a strong wind!

"My, my!" the poor lady yelled. "I must turn my back to this wind. I must keep my hat on my head."

Though North Wind kept huffing and puffing with all its might, the lady held her hat tighter and tighter.

North Wind could not blow any more. The lady would not let her hat fly off.

"I'm finished," sighed North Wind. "That's all I can do. Let's see how clever Sun is!"

Sun smiled and rose higher in the sky. Sun was silent. It shined and shined.

Robins chirped in branches in the shadow of a big tree. Lemons hid from the heat under tree leaves. Spiders also sat in shade.

"My, my! It is so hot," said the lady.

Sun kept shining brighter and brighter, and hotter and hotter. First, the lady took off her coat. Sun smiled when it saw that, and it burned even hotter.

"My, my! That sun is hot," sighed the lady.
She reached up, took off her hat, and sat under
the shade of a big tree.

"That's better," she sighed.

North Wind had finished puffing hard, and
Sun had finished burning hot.

"Sun wins the contest," sighed North Wind.
"Sun, how did you do it?"

"I did not give up," said Sun. "And I did not use force. Force will not help you win."

North Wind and Sun became silent. The lady, the robins, and the spiders had a picnic by a stream. It turned into a nice day.

The Telephone Call

By Jack Prelutsky

I was mad and I was sad
and I was all upset,
I couldn't go outside to play,
The weather was too wet.
But then my best friend called me up
With lots of things to say,
We made each other giggle,
I felt better right away.
When you can't think of things to do
And the rain won't ever end,
It's nice to have a telephone
to share things with your friend.

My New Words

cloud

A **cloud** floats high in the sky.

funnel

A **funnel** cloud is narrow at the bottom and wide at the top. It forms during a tornado.

head

Your **head** is where your eyes, ears, nose, mouth, and brain are.

large

Something that is **large** is big.

poor

This **poor** child is hurt.

though

Though it looked like rain, we went on our walk.

umbrella

You hold an **umbrella** over your head to keep dry when it rains.

wash

When you **wash** something, you clean it with soap and water. To **wash** away means to carry along by water.

Acknowledgments

Poetry

34 "My Favorite Things" Copyright © 1959 by Richard Rodgers and Oscar Hammerstein II. Copyright Renewed *Williamson Music* owner of publication and allied rights throughout the World. International Copyright Secured. All Rights Reserved.

158 "The Telephone Call" from *Rainy Rainy Saturday* by Jack Prelutsky. Copyright © 1980 by Jack Prelutsky.

Illustrations

4, 5, 22–32 David Opie; **34** Stacey Schuett; **37, 52–60** Adam Gustavson; **96–105** Kathryn Mitter; **112–122** Mary Rojas

Photographs

Every effort has been made to secure permission and provide appropriate credit for photographic material. The publisher deeply regrets any omission and pledges to correct errors called to its attention in subsequent editions.

Unless otherwise acknowledged, all photographs are the property of Scott Foresman, a division of Pearson Education.

Photo locators denoted as follows: Top (T), Center (C), Bottom (B), Left (L), Right (R), Background (Bkgd).

5 ©Arthur Tilley/Getty Images; **6** Brand X Pictures; **8** ©Tom McCarthy/PhotoEdit; **9** ©WR Publishing/Alamy; **10** Getty Images; **12** (Bkgd) ©Cathy Melloan, (TL) ©Tom Stewart/Corbis, (CL) ©Yellow Dog Productions/Getty Images, (TC) ©Allig/Getty Images, (TR, C) ©Royalty-Free/Corbis, (BR) ©Ariel Skelley/Corbis; **13** (TL) ©MedioImages/Getty Images, (CL) ©Stephen Simpson/Getty Images, (CR) ©James Schnepf/Getty Images, (TR) ©Royalty-Free/Corbis; **14** Jim Whitmer; **15** (TC) ©Francis G. Mayer/Corbis, (C) Getty Images; **16** ©David Lees/Corbis; **17** ©Bettmann/Corbis; **18** ©Michael Freeman/Corbis; **19** (C) The Granger Collection, NY, (BR) ©Bettmann/Corbis, (CR) Stockdisc; **20** (TL) Getty Images, (TR) Stockdisc, (C) ©Yuriko Nakao/Reuters/Corbis, (BL) ©Photolibrary Pty. Ltd./Index Open, (BR) ©Jonathan Nourok/PhotoEdit; **21** (TC) ©Ariel Skelley/Corbis, (BL) ©Arthur Tilley/Getty Images, (BR) ©Mel Yates/Getty Images; **36** (TL) ©Cathy Melloan, (C) Geoff Dann/©DK Images; **37** ©Cathy Melloan; **38** (TL) ©Plainpicture/Endless Image/Alamy Images, (CL) ©Royalty-Free/Corbis; **40** ©DK Images; **41** ©Thomas Dodge/Corbis; **42** ©Owen Franken/Corbis; **43** ©Eric Gaillard/Reuters/Corbis; **44** ©Photolibrary Pty. Ltd./Index Open; **45** (T) ©Royalty-Free/Corbis, (CL) Ian O'Leary/©DK Images; **46** ©Cathy Melloan; **47** (T) ©Royalty-Free/Corbis, (CL) Stockdisc; **48** ©Cathy Melloan; **49** (T) Alistair Duncan/©DK Images, (CL) Geoff Dann/©DK Images; **50** ©Bryan Mullennix/Alamy Images; **51** (T) ©Danny Gawlowski/Dallas Morning News/Corbis, (CL) ©DK Images; **64** ©Keren Su/Danita Delimont, Agent; **65** (TR) ©Peter Steiner/Alamy Images, (CR) Courtesy of Dr. O. Lynne Nelson, College of Veterinary Medicine, Washington State University; **66** (C) ©Getty Images, (CL) ©Peter Steiner/Alamy Images; **67** ©Roy Morsch/Corbis; **68** (C) ©Joel Sartore/Getty Images, (CL) ©Heidi & Hans-Jurgen Koch/Minden Pictures; **69** ©Lynn Stone/Animals Animals/Earth Scenes; **70** (C) ©Keren Su/Danita Delimont, Agent, (CL) ©Gerry Ellis/Globio/Minden Pictures; **71** ©Keren Su/Danita Delimont, Agent; **72** (C) ©Martin Harvey/Corbis, (CL) ©Gerry Ellis/Globio/Minden Pictures; **73** ©David Samuel Robbins/Corbis; **74** ©Danny Lehman/Corbis; **76** ©Galen Rowell/Corbis; **77** ©Joe McDonald/Corbis; **78** (Bkgd) ©Royalty-Free/Corbis, (CL, CR) Courtesy of Dr. O. Lynne Nelson, College of Veterinary Medicine, Washington State University; **79** (CL, CR) Courtesy of Dr. O. Lynne Nelson, College of Veterinary Medicine, Washington State University; **80** ©John Conrad/Corbis; **94** (TCL) ©Jeff Vanuga/Corbis, (TCR, BCL, BR, Bkgd) Getty Images; **97** ©Rich LaSalle/Getty Images; **106** The Granger Collection, NY; **108** (C) ©Bettmann/Corbis, (TL) North Wind Picture Archives; **110** Corbis; **111** (TR) North Wind Picture Archives, (CR) ©Rich LaSalle/Getty Images; **126** ©Cathy Melloan/PhotoEdit; **128** ©Giampiero Sposito/Reuters/Corbis; **130** ©Jim Reed/Corbis; **131** ©Weatherstock/Omni Photo Communications; **132** ©Ryan McVay/Getty Images; **134** (Bkgd) Corbis, (C) ©Cathy Melloan/PhotoEdit; **135** (C) ©Enigma/Alamy, (TR) ©Lon C. Diehl/PhotoEdit; **136** (L, CR, Bkgd) Getty Images, (CL) ©Jane Faircloth/Transparencies, Inc., (R) ©Michael Boys/Corbis; **137** (C) Getty Images, (CR) ©Rob Atkins/Getty Images; **138** ©Jane Faircloth/Transparencies, Inc.; **140** ©Lisa M. Robinson/Getty Images; **142** ©Herbert Kehrer/Zefa/Corbis; **144** (L, CR, Bkgd) Getty Images, (CL) ©Jane Faircloth/Transparencies, Inc., (R) ©Michael Boys/Corbis; **145** (C) Getty Images, (CC) ©Rob Atkins/Getty Images